Ease the Tease

Judy S. Freedman and Mimi P. Black

Illustrated by Steve Mark

Library of Congress Cataloging-in-Publication Data
Names: Freedman, Judy S., author. | Black, Mimi, author. | Mark, Steve, illustrator.
Title: Ease the tease! / by Judy S. Freedman, M.S.W., L.C.S.W. and Mimi P. Black, Ph.D. ; illustrated by Steve Mark.
Description: Minneapolis, MN : Free Spirit Publishing, 2021. | Series: Little Laugh & Learn | Audience: Ages 6–9
Identifiers: LCCN 2020050780 (print) | LCCN 2020050781 (ebook) | ISBN 9781631983504 (paperback) | ISBN 9781631983511 (pdf) | ISBN 9781631983528 (epub)
Subjects: LCSH: Teasing—Juvenile literature.
Classification: LCC BF637.T43 F74 2020 (print) | LCC BF637.T43 (ebook) | DDC 158.2—dc23
LC record available at https://lccn.loc.gov/2020050780
LC ebook record available at https://lccn.loc.gov/2020050781

Edited by Eric Braun
Cover and interior design by Emily Dyer

Printed by: 584728
Printed In: India
PO#: 15817

Free Spirit Publishing
An imprint of Teacher Created Materials
9850 51st Avenue North, Suite 100
Minneapolis, MN 55442
(612) 338-2068
help4kids@freespirit.com
freespirit.com

Ease
the
Tease

CONTENTS

The Terrible, Troublesome Truth About Teasing

Has anyone ever called you names or said mean things to you?

Teasing. It happens to lots and lots (and lots!) of kids.

Every day.

Sometimes people tease in a friendly way. Fun and friendly teasing is when one person **has fun with** another person. It's a way of joking and kidding around that makes everyone smile or laugh.

Sometimes teasing is *meant* to be friendly . . . but feels hurtful.

Sometimes teasing isn't meant to be friendly at all. Mean teasing is when someone **makes fun of** someone else. Maybe they call them mean names or laugh at them.

This kind of teasing is wrong. Sadly, it still happens. Sometimes kids don't even realize it's wrong!

What Hurtful Teasing Sounds Like

Kids can be teased about . . .

what they do

- "You are such a slow runner. I wish you weren't on my team."
- "Your voice is so annoying."

how they look

- "Fatso."
- "Your hair is weird."

their feelings

- "Scaredy-cat."
- "What a crybaby."

their schoolwork

- "Nerd."
- "Can't you read?"

their friends

- "Why do you like Maria? She is such a loser."
- "You hang out with the geeks."

what they like

- "Your lunch is gross!"
- "That game is for babies."

Kids can be teased about . . .

✔ **their family**

- "Weirdo! You have two moms."
- "Your parents don't even speak English."

✔ **their names**

- "Stinkin' Lincoln."
- "Mary, Mary, hairy and scary."

their differences

- "Your accent is dumb."
- "Joey, why do you like girls' games?"

anything (even if it's not true)

- "Dog breath."
- "Butthead."

What Hurtful Teasing Feels Like

Mean teasing can hurt. It can feel embarrassing.

When you're teased, you might feel angry. Maybe you even feel like you'll explode.

You might feel sad. You might feel scared.

You might even feel smaller than you really are.

You can't control what someone else says or does. But if you've been teased, here's **good news**.

You *can* control how you react to it. Your reaction may be able to **ease** the teasing. You can make it happen less often, or maybe even end it.

You might even be able to change how you feel about teasing. Then it won't bother you as much.

Now that would be powerful.

QUESTION:
What if I have teased people?

If you've ever teased someone, there's good news for you too.

It's not too late to apologize for hurting their feelings. Even better, you can promise not to do it again.

Remember how it feels to be teased. That can help keep you from teasing others.

What NOT to Do When You're Teased

When kids tease, they want to see you get upset.

When you get upset, they feel powerful. That kind of power may feel good to them.

SCHOOL

Upset Reactions to Avoid

Kids who are teased might show they are upset in different ways.

Sometimes they might get angry. They may try to tease back. They may even hit the person who teased them.

Whoa, there! Is this really such a good idea?

Nope. Kids who show anger are giving the kids teasing them what they're looking for: an upset reaction. Getting upset will probably lead to more teasing. It might even lead to other bad things, like getting hurt or in trouble.

Other kids feel very sad and hurt when they are teased. They may cry.

What do you think of this idea? Is crying going to stop the teasing?

Double nope. Crying can lead to more teasing. But boy, it's hard to keep from crying sometimes.

Some kids feel very afraid when they're teased. They may show this fear with their faces, words, or bodies. Or all three!

Bet you can guess the answer to this one. Does a scared reaction help?

Triple nope. Kids who are teasing like to see a scared reaction. They'll likely keep teasing.

Yipe
Scared words
Big, Scared eyes
Scared mouth
Scared posture
Scared fumbling hands
Shaky knees

So What's a Kid to Do?

Even more good news.

Keep reading to learn not one . . . not two . . . but *ten* helpful ways to **ease the tease**.

These tools can help you keep your cool, even when you're feeling hot inside. And so . . .

Ta-da!

You don't give the teasing kids the reactions they're looking for.

QUESTION:

Wait! I don't even think I could try ONE way. How can I learn TEN?

Don't worry! Later in this book, you'll find great ideas for practicing these tools with a trusted grown-up. (It might even be fun!)

You don't need to learn all ten, especially not right away. You might find just one or two that work well for you. Or maybe you'll master more! But even one will help.

CHAPTER 3

Two Ways to Ease the Tease with Pure Brainpower

The first two tease-easers are things you can *think*. They help you keep your cool. They remind you that mean words are not nearly as powerful as your amazing mind.

Tool 1: Use Self-Talk

Self-Talk is silently saying things in your mind that help you stay cool. Your words can help you feel stronger. They can keep you from showing that you're upset.

Here are some examples of self-talk.

"Even though I don't like this teasing, I can handle it. It's not the end of the world."

"I'm really tired of being teased because I'm having a hard time with math. But I'm not going to get mad. Lots of great people have had a hard time with math."

Thinking nice thoughts about yourself can help you feel strong and brave. It can help you calm your anger and hold back your tears. You'll show the kids who are teasing you that they don't have any power over you.

Here are some self-talk ideas.

- Remind yourself of something you're good at. For example, "I am really funny. Lots of kids like hanging out with me."
- Say to yourself, "I like who I am."
- Boost yourself up. "I'm too cool to let mean words bug me."

Tool 2: Use Imagination Power

In this tease-easer, you **Imagine** ways to get rid of the teasing words. Think of it as your brain's chance to *zap* the words you're hearing. That way they can't get anywhere near your feelings.

You might imagine that the words are bouncing off you. Or you can pretend you have a shield that protects you from bad words and put-downs. Or you can imagine ways to make the words disappear. *Poof!*

Your brain loves doing stuff like this. Here are some fun imagining ideas. What others can you think of? You can even draw what you're imagining.

- Hit the teasing words with a baseball bat.
- Power kick the mean words away.
- Throw those words in the garbage can.
- Be an artist and paint right over the tease.
- Flip the teases away like a gymnast.
- Flush the words down the toilet.

Mean
words

Three Ways to Ease the Tease Right Away

The strategies in this chapter are things you can *do* or *say*. Use these in the moment when someone is teasing you.

They can help you feel **stronger** and keep your **cool**.

Tool 3: Ignore the Teasing

Showing that you're angry, sad, or afraid can make the teasing worse. You might want to try to **Ignore the Teasing**. That means you do not talk to people when they're teasing you. You don't even look at them. Ignoring means acting as if the teasing isn't happening at all.

If possible, walk away from the teasing. Join others if you can.

This tease-easer is like the others. It works because you don't have an upset reaction. You don't give any reaction at all!

Can you think of some ways a person's body and face look when they're *not* upset? Try some out right now.

Tool 4: Say "So?"

This tease-easer is so simple that it's just one calm word: **So?**

If someone teases you, reply with a calm, cool, "So?" It's even better with an I-don't-care shrug of your shoulders.

Most people will get the message that you're too cool to get upset. Then they give up. Score one for you!

Other quick and easy responses:

Yeah, right.

Whatever.

Who cares?

Tool 5: Use an I-Message

Sometimes an **I-Message** is all you need. It's a three-step way to stick up for yourself. You tell the other person:

- How you feel
- Why you feel that way
- What you would like them to do

The I-message shows the person teasing you that you're strong enough to know you deserve better.

Look at the person and speak clearly and politely.

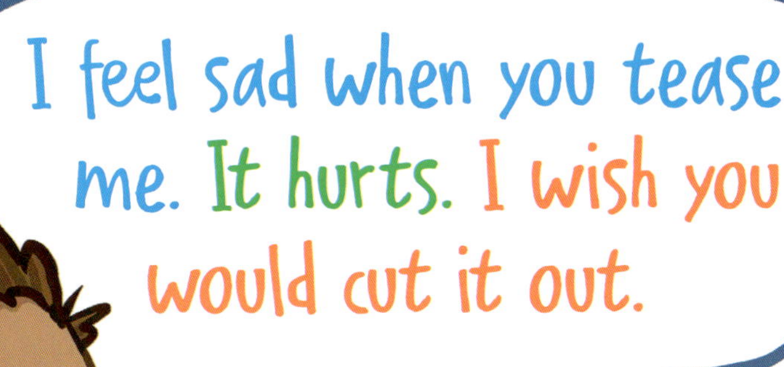

I get mad when you say that. It's mean. Knock it off.

It's important to know that the I-message *doesn't* work very well in some situations. After all, you're saying that the teasing has reached your feelings.

Here is when the I-message works best:

- There is a grown-up nearby to hear what you're saying. It's their clue that you're being spoken to in a mean way—but you're not losing your cool over it. Good for you. Even better, the person teasing you gets a clue that a grown-up may be listening. The teasing's more likely to stop.

- The person teasing you is a friend. Friends care how you feel. They're likely to stop teasing if they know it's bothering you.

CHAPTER 5

Four Ways to Ease the Tease . . . with Surprise!

The tools in this chapter are a little trickier. They may take some extra practice. But they can be great ways to ease the tease because they catch the other person off guard.

Tool 6: Agree with the Facts

Sometimes someone might tease you by pointing out something they think is strange or different. You can surprise them if you **Agree with the Facts**. They might think their words are mean. But you know it's no big deal.

Tease: "So weird that you're the only girl on the hockey team."
Response: "That's true, I'm the only girl on the team."

• • •

Tease: "You talk really funny."
Response: "Yes, I have an accent."

• • •

Tease: "You're the shortest kid in the class."

Response: "Yep!"

Here are some other ways to neatly agree with the tease:

Just make sure you stand up straight, look the person in the eye, and speak calmly and confidently. This will often end the conversation. What else is there to say?

Tool 7: Take the Tease as a Compliment

You can respond as if the tease is the *opposite* of an insult. That takes the sting out of it.

Tease: "You're such a geek."
Response: "Hey, thanks!"

• • •

Tease: "Boys don't wear nail polish."
Response: "That's nice that you pay so much attention to my nails. I'll wear blue tomorrow!"

• • •

Tease: "Why are you wearing another ugly shirt?"

Response: "Thanks for noticing what I wear every day!"

You might enjoy trying other responses like "Oooo, thanks!"

Just keep your cool when you respond, and the teasing doesn't stand much of a chance. You've cut the **fun** out of making fun.

Tool 8: Give a Compliment

The person teasing you is expecting you to get angry, sad, or afraid. Sometimes you may be too mad to try this one, and that's okay. But imagine the person's surprise when you smile and **Give a Compliment** instead.

Tease: "You loser! You struck out again!"
Response: "I wish I could hit the ball like you can. You're a great baseball player."

• • •

Tease: "Your shoes are *so* not cool."
Response: "I keep meaning to tell you how much I like *your* shoes. Where did you get them?"

Sometimes people get so busy enjoying your compliment that they completely forget about teasing you.

Tool 9: Use Humor

This can be a fun way to ease the tease. It's even fun to practice. Use **Humor** to turn the mean words into a setup for a joke. Instead of getting upset, you can say something funny. You can even just laugh!

Tease: "You have so many freckles!"
Response: "Sometimes I play connect-the-dots."

• • •

Tease: "You have huge ears . . . they look like wings!"
Response: "Yeah, I can hear the ice cream truck from miles away."

• • •

Tease: "Why are you always last to finish?"

Response: "I come from a family of snails."

Usually people are surprised by this reaction. They don't expect you to laugh or make a joke when they tease you. Score another one for you.

But hey, don't forget that your humor should be about yourself or the tease. It wouldn't be cool to make fun of someone else, even the person teasing you.

Don't worry if you can't think of something funny to say. Just a simple smile, laugh, or cheerful "you crack me up" can work.

When the Teasing Gets Worse and Worse

Sometimes you try different ways to ease the tease, but kids keep teasing you. Teasing that happens over and over again is bullying. Someone might even hurt you or threaten to hurt you. That's also bullying, even if they tell you they're "just teasing." It's not safe, and it's not okay.

In these situations, you have one very important tool you can use.

Tool 10: Ask for Help

In these situations, find an adult you trust and **Ask for Help**. You can ask a parent, grandparent, teacher, or family friend. You can ask a counselor, social worker, religious leader, or other caring adult.

"These kids make fun of the way I talk. I've asked them to stop but they won't. They follow me around and copy me. Can you help?"

Reporting to a grown-up is not tattling. It is the right thing to do to keep yourself safe.

The Power of Practice

Wow! That's ten powerful ways to ease those teases.

And here's the **best news** of all. These tease-easers are all *skills*. Most skills get better with practice, even if they seem tough at first.

Use Self-Talk
Use Imagination Power
Ignore the Teasing
Say "So?"
Use an I-Message
Agree with the Facts
Take the Tease as a Compliment
Use Humor
Give a Compliment
Ask for Help

Find a trusted grown-up and ask them to read this book with you. They can help you practice.

The adult can pretend to tease you, and you can try out responses. Which responses make you look and sound like you're keeping your cool? Which ones feel the most comfortable?

A trusted adult can help you think of more tease-easing responses too.

CHAPTER 8

Ease the Tease . . . with Teamwork

You can teach others how to ease the tease too. Then you can ask them to help you spread the word.

When you see or hear teasing, it's important to stand up—and **Speak Up**—instead of standing by.

Wow, look at that—you've created your own *We*-Message!

We don't like it when you talk that way. We don't use hurtful words.

Ease the Tease
Ease the Tease
Ease the Tease
Ease the Tease
Ease the Tease

When kids act together, they have a lot of power to end teasing and bullying. That's because *most* people think being mean is uncool. That means most people are on your side.

Team up to ease the tease at your school, in your neighborhood, and anywhere you see or hear teasing.

Now **that's** powerful!

GLOSSARY

apologize: to say that you are sorry about something

bullying: threatening or hurting someone or trying to make someone feel unsafe

compliment: to say something nice about someone

ignore: to pay no attention to something

reaction: the way you respond with your words or your body to someone's words or actions

self-talk: words you say to yourself in your mind

About the Authors and Illustrator

Judy S. Freedman, M.S.W., L.C.S.W., a licensed clinical social worker, created the Easing the Teasing program, which empowers elementary-age kids with essential skills to handle teasing incidents. This was the basis for her parenting book *Easing the Teasing: Helping Your Child Cope with Name-Calling, Ridicule, and Verbal Bullying* (Contemporary Books/McGraw Hill). Judy received the Illinois School Social Worker of the Year Award in 2011. She lives in suburban Chicago with her husband.

Mimi P. Black, Ph.D., is a psychologist, bullying prevention specialist, and actor. She has published articles on developmental psychology topics and given invited addresses on bullying prevention to school administrators, faculty, parents, and students. An on-camera and voice actor for many years, Mimi has also has worked on both sides of the camera in the development of children's educational television programs. She lives in Chicagoland with her family.

Steve Mark is a freelance illustrator and a part-time puppeteer. He lives in Minnesota and is the father of three and the husband of one. Steve has illustrated many books for children, including *Ease the Tease!* from the Little Laugh & Learn® series and all the books in the Laugh & Learn® series for older kids.